There's No Doubt About It

Stay on that number–don't make a move.
Stay on that number–there's none to remove.
Stay on that number–for the answer, you see,
is the same number. It's so easy!

TRACK 1

1	2	3	4	5	6
−0	−0	−0	−0	−0	−0

7	8	9	10	11	12
−0	−0	−0	−0	−0	−0

"the answer stays the same.
the answer will remain."

There's no doubt about it–the answer stays the same.
There's no doubt about it–the answer will remain.
For when you are subtracting, and a zero you see,
to figure out the answer is so easy!

Solve.

13	18	9	3	12	7
−0	−0	−0	−0	−0	−0

15	2	8	16	4	17
−0	−0	−0	−0	−0	−0

The Answer Is Zero Every Time

The answer is zero every time.
The answer is zero–this is not a line.
The answer is zero–yes, it's true.
Any number minus itself is always zero–
this is a subtraction rule!

Solve.

$$
\begin{array}{r} 1 \\ -1 \\ \hline \end{array}
\qquad
\begin{array}{r} 2 \\ -2 \\ \hline \end{array}
\qquad
\begin{array}{r} 3 \\ -3 \\ \hline \end{array}
\qquad
\begin{array}{r} 4 \\ -4 \\ \hline \end{array}
\qquad
\begin{array}{r} 5 \\ -5 \\ \hline \end{array}
\qquad
\begin{array}{r} 6 \\ -6 \\ \hline \end{array}
$$

$$
\begin{array}{r} 7 \\ -7 \\ \hline \end{array}
\qquad
\begin{array}{r} 8 \\ -8 \\ \hline \end{array}
\qquad
\begin{array}{r} 9 \\ -9 \\ \hline \end{array}
\qquad
\begin{array}{r} 10 \\ -10 \\ \hline \end{array}
\qquad
\begin{array}{r} 11 \\ -11 \\ \hline \end{array}
\qquad
\begin{array}{r} 12 \\ -12 \\ \hline \end{array}
$$

There's no doubt about it–the answer stays the same.
There's no doubt about it–the answer will remain.
For when you are subtracting, and a zero you see,
to figure out the answer is so easy!

Solve.

$$
\begin{array}{r} 42 \\ -42 \\ \hline \end{array}
\qquad
\begin{array}{r} 63 \\ -63 \\ \hline \end{array}
\qquad
\begin{array}{r} 107 \\ -107 \\ \hline \end{array}
\qquad
\begin{array}{r} 894 \\ -894 \\ \hline \end{array}
\qquad
\begin{array}{r} 3{,}261 \\ -3{,}261 \\ \hline \end{array}
$$

YOU GOT IT!
Any number minus itself is always…

One Less

Write the number that is one less. Subtract.

TRACK 3

18 – _17_ = ____   9 – ____ = ____

17 – ____ = ____   8 – ____ = ____

16 – ____ = ____   7 – ____ = ____

15 – ____ = ____   6 – ____ = ____

14 – ____ = ____   5 – ____ = ____

13 – ____ = ____   4 – ____ = ____

12 – ____ = ____   3 – ____ = ____

11 – ____ = ____   2 – ____ = ____

10 – ____ = ____   1 – ____ = ____

Countdown Strategy:
If you're subtracting one, just count down one!

-1
-3
-5
-2
-4
-1
-3
-2
-4
-5
-1

3

-0, -1, Same Number

1 − 0	2 − 0	3 − 0	4 − 0	5 − 0
6 − 1	7 − 1	8 − 1	9 − 1	10 − 1
5 − 1	4 − 1	3 − 1	2 − 1	1 − 1
10 − 0	9 − 0	8 − 0	7 − 0	6 − 0
10 − 10	13 − 13	16 − 16	11 − 11	18 − 18

Subtraction Practice

Write the missing number in the circle.

$$3 - \bigcirc = 3 \qquad \bigcirc - 4 = 1 \qquad 1 - \bigcirc = 0 \qquad 2 - 2 = \bigcirc \qquad 4 - \bigcirc = 2$$

$$\bigcirc - 3 = 2 \qquad 5 - \bigcirc = 4 \qquad 1 - 1 = \bigcirc \qquad \bigcirc - 3 = 1 \qquad 2 - \bigcirc = 0$$

$$5 - \bigcirc = 3 \qquad \bigcirc - 4 = 1 \qquad 3 - 2 = \bigcirc \qquad \bigcirc - 3 = 2 \qquad 5 - \bigcirc = 0$$

$$\bigcirc - 2 = 2 \qquad 3 - \bigcirc = 0 \qquad \bigcirc - 3 = 1 \qquad 5 - \bigcirc = 1 \qquad 4 - 2 = \bigcirc$$

5

Minuends 1, 2, 3, 4, 5

$$\boxed{} - 2 = 3$$
$$\boxed{} - 5 = 0$$
$$1 - \boxed{} = 1$$
$$3 - \boxed{} = 2$$
$$\boxed{} - 2 = 2$$

$$2 - \boxed{} = 1$$
$$\boxed{} - 2 = 2$$
$$5 - \boxed{} = 1$$
$$3 - \boxed{} = 0$$
$$2 - \boxed{} = 0$$

$$\boxed{} - 4 = 1$$
$$\boxed{} - 2 = 1$$
$$4 - \boxed{} = 2$$
$$3 - \boxed{} = 3$$
$$2 - \boxed{} = 1$$

$$\boxed{} - 5 = 0$$
$$\boxed{} - 1 = 0$$
$$1 - \boxed{} = 1$$
$$2 - \boxed{} = 1$$
$$\boxed{} - 3 = 2$$

$$\boxed{} - 4 = 1$$
$$3 - \boxed{} = 0$$
$$2 - \boxed{} = 1$$
$$4 - \boxed{} = 3$$
$$5 - \boxed{} = 2$$

Minuends 1, 2, 3, 4, 5   TRACK

1 −1	2 −1	2 −2	3 −1	3 −2
5 −2	5 −1	5 −3	5 −4	5 −5
2 −1	2 −2	2 −0	4 −2	5 −2
4 −2	4 −3	4 −1	4 −4	4 −0
3 −2	3 −1	3 −3	3 −0	5 −0

7

3 −1 = **2**	2 −1	2 −2	3 −2	1 −1
3 −3	4 −1	4 −2	4 −3	4 −4
5 −1	5 −2	5 −3	5 −4	5 −5

Problem Search

Subtract and write the difference. Find and circle the subtraction facts in the puzzle.

4 −2

3	−	1	=	2	1	−	0	5	2
−	5	−	5	=	0	4	3	1	−
3	−	2	=	1	1	−	4	−	1
=	5	=	0	4	4	5	=	1	=
4	1	−	4	−	3	−	3	=	1
−	5	2	=	3	−	3	=	0	2
4	5	−	2	=	3	=	−	1	3
−	3	2	−	1	−	5	=	5	=
4	−	=	3	−	=	−	2	−	4
=	−	0	4	5	1	3	5	4	3
0	0	=	4	−	1	=	3	=	1
5	−	1	=	4	−	2	3	1	=
2	4	−	2	=	2	5	=	2	3

Minuends 6, 7

6 −1	6 −3	6 −2	6 −4	6 −5
7 −2	7 −1	7 −3	7 −4	7 −5
6 −1	6 −2	7 −0	6 −4	7 −5
7 −6	7 −7	6 −5	7 −3	6 −6
6 −2	7 −4	7 −1	6 −0	7 −0

9

Race To The Center

Practice the subtraction facts 0 – 7. Say each subtraction sentence and the difference. Predict how quickly you can move to the center. Set a timer and discover how well you know subtraction facts!

6 – 0	7 – 1	6 – 3	4 – 1	3 – 3	2 – 2	7 – 2	5 – 3	4 – 2	3 – 1
7 – 4	5 – 3	4 – 4	1 – 0	4 – 1	7 – 6	5 – 1	6 – 4	5 – 2	7 – 7
5 – 2	4 – 3	5 – 1	6 – 6	7 – 5	3 – 2	4 – 0	3 – 1	2 – 1	6 – 5
7 – 3	4 – 2	7 – 5	7 – 7	2 – 1	5 – 2	5 – 5	7 – 6	4 – 3	4 – 2
1 – 1	6 – 3	2 – 1	2 – 2	6 – 2	★	6 – 4	7 – 1	5 – 0	4 – 3
4 – 2	3 – 3	6 – 4	7 – 5	4 – 1	7 – 7	6 – 5	2 – 1	4 – 2	5 – 5
6 – 0	5 – 1	5 – 2	6 – 4	7 – 1	6 – 5	2 – 2	5 – 3	2 – 1	4 – 3
7 – 7	3 – 2	5 – 2	6 – 2	3 – 1	5 – 3	4 – 2	7 – 4	7 – 2	5 – 4
4 – 3	7 – 0	5 – 5	4 – 2	5 – 5	6 – 3	3 – 1	4 – 3	5 – 2	6 – 4
6 – 2	5 – 3	4 – 3	5 – 2	7 – 1	7 – 5	4 – 1	3 – 2	1 – 1	1 – 0
5 – 0	6 – 4	7 – 3	5 – 5	3 – 1	2 – 2	1 – 0	6 – 6	5 – 2	7 – 5
4 – 2	5 – 2	7 – 0	5 – 3	5 – 1	6 – 3	7 – 6	6 – 0	4 – 2	2 – 1

Minuends 8, 9

8 − 0	8 − 1	8 − 2	8 − 3	8 − 4
9 − 1	9 − 2	9 − 3	9 − 4	9 − 5
8 − 6	8 − 7	9 − 6	8 − 8	9 − 9
9 − 2	9 − 3	8 − 1	9 − 4	8 − 0
8 − 2	8 − 6	9 − 3	9 − 0	8 − 1

11

Minuend 10

$$\begin{array}{r} 10 \\ -\ 0 \\ \hline \end{array} \qquad \begin{array}{r} 10 \\ -\ 1 \\ \hline \end{array} \qquad \begin{array}{r} 10 \\ -\ 2 \\ \hline \end{array} \qquad \begin{array}{r} 10 \\ -\ 3 \\ \hline \end{array} \qquad \begin{array}{r} 10 \\ -\ 4 \\ \hline \end{array}$$

$$\begin{array}{r} 10 \\ -\ 5 \\ \hline \end{array} \qquad \begin{array}{r} 10 \\ -\ 6 \\ \hline \end{array} \qquad \begin{array}{r} 10 \\ -\ 7 \\ \hline \end{array} \qquad \begin{array}{r} 10 \\ -\ 8 \\ \hline \end{array} \qquad \begin{array}{r} 10 \\ -\ 9 \\ \hline \end{array}$$

$$\begin{array}{r} 10 \\ -\ 1 \\ \hline \end{array} \qquad \begin{array}{r} 10 \\ -\ 4 \\ \hline \end{array} \qquad \begin{array}{r} 10 \\ -\ 0 \\ \hline \end{array} \qquad \begin{array}{r} 10 \\ -\ 2 \\ \hline \end{array} \qquad \begin{array}{r} 10 \\ -\ 10 \\ \hline \end{array}$$

$$\begin{array}{r} 10 \\ -\ 7 \\ \hline \end{array} \qquad \begin{array}{r} 10 \\ -\ 9 \\ \hline \end{array} \qquad \begin{array}{r} 10 \\ -\ 3 \\ \hline \end{array} \qquad \begin{array}{r} 10 \\ -\ 5 \\ \hline \end{array} \qquad \begin{array}{r} 10 \\ -\ 8 \\ \hline \end{array}$$

$$\begin{array}{r} 10 \\ -\ 10 \\ \hline \end{array} \qquad \begin{array}{r} 10 \\ -\ 5 \\ \hline \end{array} \qquad \begin{array}{r} 10 \\ -\ 7 \\ \hline \end{array} \qquad \begin{array}{r} 10 \\ -\ 4 \\ \hline \end{array} \qquad \begin{array}{r} 10 \\ -\ 1 \\ \hline \end{array}$$

Subtraction Practice

Write the missing number in the circle.

$$8 - \bigcirc = 5$$

$$9 - \bigcirc = 7$$

$$\bigcirc - 4 = 4$$

$$7 - 2 = \bigcirc$$

$$5 - \bigcirc = 4$$

$$3 - 2 = \bigcirc$$

$$\bigcirc - 3 = 6$$

$$8 - \bigcirc = 7$$

$$\bigcirc - 2 = 3$$

$$9 - 5 = \bigcirc$$

$$1 - \bigcirc = 1$$

$$4 - 2 = \bigcirc$$

$$\bigcirc - 3 = 3$$

$$\bigcirc - 2 = 6$$

$$7 - \bigcirc = 2$$

$$9 - \bigcirc = 0$$

$$2 - 1 = \bigcirc$$

$$\bigcirc - 3 = 4$$

$$8 - \bigcirc = 2$$

$$5 - 2 = \bigcirc$$

13

Left margin (vertical):

Bowling By Subtraction

Write the difference.

10	10	10	10	10	10	10	10	10	10	10
- 0	- 1	- 2	- 3	- 4	- 5	- 6	- 7	- 8	- 9	- 10

Pretend you're bowling. Complete the subtraction sentence for each roll. Each red pin will be knocked down. How many will be left standing?

10 - ___ = ___

10 - ___ = ___

10 - ___ = ___

10 - ___ = ___

10 - ___ = ___

10 - ___ = ___

10 - ___ = ___

10 - ___ = ___

10 - ___ = ___

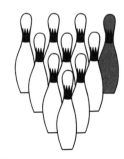
10 - ___ = ___

10 - ___ = ___

14

Minuend 11

$$\begin{array}{r} 11 \\ -\ 0 \\ \hline \end{array} \qquad \begin{array}{r} 11 \\ -\ 1 \\ \hline \end{array} \qquad \begin{array}{r} 11 \\ -\ 2 \\ \hline \end{array} \qquad \begin{array}{r} 11 \\ -\ 3 \\ \hline \end{array} \qquad \begin{array}{r} 11 \\ -\ 4 \\ \hline \end{array}$$

$$\begin{array}{r} 11 \\ -10 \\ \hline \end{array} \qquad \begin{array}{r} 11 \\ -11 \\ \hline \end{array} \qquad \begin{array}{r} 11 \\ -\ 3 \\ \hline \end{array} \qquad \begin{array}{r} 11 \\ -\ 4 \\ \hline \end{array} \qquad \begin{array}{r} 11 \\ -\ 9 \\ \hline \end{array}$$

$$\begin{array}{r} 11 \\ -\ 5 \\ \hline \end{array} \qquad \begin{array}{r} 11 \\ -\ 2 \\ \hline \end{array} \qquad \begin{array}{r} 11 \\ -\ 1 \\ \hline \end{array} \qquad \begin{array}{r} 11 \\ -\ 3 \\ \hline \end{array} \qquad \begin{array}{r} 11 \\ -\ 6 \\ \hline \end{array}$$

$$\begin{array}{r} 11 \\ -\ 9 \\ \hline \end{array} \qquad \begin{array}{r} 11 \\ -\ 7 \\ \hline \end{array} \qquad \begin{array}{r} 11 \\ -\ 6 \\ \hline \end{array} \qquad \begin{array}{r} 11 \\ -\ 2 \\ \hline \end{array} \qquad \begin{array}{r} 11 \\ -\ 5 \\ \hline \end{array}$$

$$\begin{array}{r} 11 \\ -\ 3 \\ \hline \end{array} \qquad \begin{array}{r} 11 \\ -10 \\ \hline \end{array} \qquad \begin{array}{r} 11 \\ -\ 2 \\ \hline \end{array} \qquad \begin{array}{r} 11 \\ -\ 0 \\ \hline \end{array} \qquad \begin{array}{r} 11 \\ -\ 4 \\ \hline \end{array}$$

Number Line Subtraction

Finish drawing each subtraction sentence on the number line.
Write the missing subtrahend.

0   1   2   3   4   5   6   7   8   9   10   11   12   13

11 - _7_ **= 4**

0   1   2   3   4   5   6   7   8   9   10   11   12   13

8 - ____ **= 3**

0   1   2   3   4   5   6   7   8   9   10   11   12   13

10 - ____ **= 8**

0   1   2   3   4   5   6   7   8   9   10   11   12   13

9 - ____ **= 5**

0   1   2   3   4   5   6   7   8   9   10   11   12   13

11 - ____ **= 8**

0   1   2   3   4   5   6   7   8   9   10   11   12   13

8 - ____ **= 4**

0   1   2   3   4   5   6   7   8   9   10   11   12   13

9 - ____ **= 7**

0   1   2   3   4   5   6   7   8   9   10   11   12   13

10 - ____ **= 3**

Minuends 12, 13

12	12	12	12	12
−0	−1	−2	−3	−4

12	12	12	12	12
−5	−6	−7	−8	−9

13	13	13	13	13
−1	−2	−4	−3	−5

13	13	13	13	13
−6	−7	−9	−8	−10

12	13	12	12	13
−10	−12	−12	−11	−13

17

©2011 Twin Sisters IP, LLC. All Rights Reserved.

Fact Families

Fact families are 3 numbers that are "related" and make 2 addition sentences and 2 subtraction sentences.
For example — 3, 4, 7:

$$\begin{array}{r} 3 \\ +4 \\ \hline 7 \end{array} \qquad \begin{array}{r} 4 \\ +3 \\ \hline 7 \end{array} \qquad \begin{array}{r} 7 \\ -4 \\ \hline 3 \end{array} \qquad \begin{array}{r} 7 \\ -3 \\ \hline 4 \end{array}$$

Fill in the missing numbers for each fact family.

Subtraction Review

-1 -2 -3 -4 -5 -6 -7 -8 -9 -10 -11 -12 -13

Row 1 left:
$$\begin{array}{r} 8 \\ +4 \\ \hline \square \end{array} \qquad \begin{array}{r} 4 \\ +8 \\ \hline \square \end{array} \qquad \begin{array}{r} 12 \\ -4 \\ \hline \square \end{array} \qquad \begin{array}{r} 12 \\ -8 \\ \hline \square \end{array}$$

Row 1 right:
$$\begin{array}{r} 6 \\ +5 \\ \hline \square \end{array} \qquad \begin{array}{r} 5 \\ +6 \\ \hline \square \end{array} \qquad \begin{array}{r} 11 \\ -5 \\ \hline \square \end{array} \qquad \begin{array}{r} 11 \\ -6 \\ \hline \square \end{array}$$

Row 2 left:
$$\begin{array}{r} \square \\ +4 \\ \hline 6 \end{array} \qquad \begin{array}{r} 4 \\ +2 \\ \hline \square \end{array} \qquad \begin{array}{r} \square \\ -4 \\ \hline 2 \end{array} \qquad \begin{array}{r} 6 \\ -\square \\ \hline 4 \end{array}$$

Row 2 right:
$$\begin{array}{r} 9 \\ +3 \\ \hline \square \end{array} \qquad \begin{array}{r} 3 \\ +\square \\ \hline 12 \end{array} \qquad \begin{array}{r} \square \\ -9 \\ \hline 3 \end{array} \qquad \begin{array}{r} 12 \\ -\square \\ \hline 9 \end{array}$$

Row 3 left:
$$\begin{array}{r} 7 \\ +3 \\ \hline \square \end{array} \qquad \begin{array}{r} \square \\ +\square \\ \hline \square \end{array} \qquad \begin{array}{r} \square \\ -\square \\ \hline \square \end{array} \qquad \begin{array}{r} \square \\ -\square \\ \hline \square \end{array}$$

Row 3 right:
$$\begin{array}{r} 6 \\ +7 \\ \hline \square \end{array} \qquad \begin{array}{r} \square \\ +\square \\ \hline \square \end{array} \qquad \begin{array}{r} \square \\ -\square \\ \hline \square \end{array} \qquad \begin{array}{r} \square \\ -\square \\ \hline \square \end{array}$$

Row 4 left:
$$\begin{array}{r} 5 \\ +2 \\ \hline \square \end{array} \qquad \begin{array}{r} \square \\ +\square \\ \hline \square \end{array} \qquad \begin{array}{r} \square \\ -\square \\ \hline \square \end{array} \qquad \begin{array}{r} \square \\ -\square \\ \hline \square \end{array}$$

Row 4 right:
$$\begin{array}{r} 8 \\ +2 \\ \hline \square \end{array} \qquad \begin{array}{r} \square \\ +\square \\ \hline \square \end{array} \qquad \begin{array}{r} \square \\ -\square \\ \hline \square \end{array} \qquad \begin{array}{r} \square \\ -\square \\ \hline \square \end{array}$$

More Fact Families

Practice Fact Families! Write the numbers in the first two squares.
Now find the third number of the fact family. Then,
write the Fact Family using those three numbers.

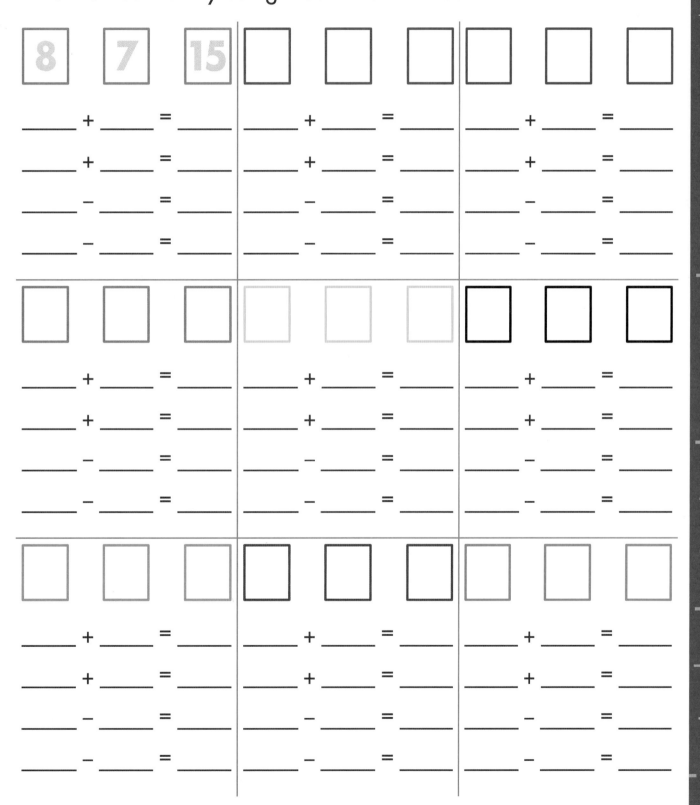

19

Minuend 14

14 − 0	14 − 1	14 − 2	14 − 3	14 − 4
14 − 5	14 − 6	14 − 7	14 − 8	14 − 9
14 − 1	14 − 4	14 − 0	14 − 2	14 − 14
14 − 7	14 − 9	14 − 3	14 − 5	14 − 8
14 − 14	14 − 5	14 − 7	14 − 4	14 − 1

Minuends 15, 16

15 − 0	15 − 1	15 − 2	15 − 3	15 − 4
15 − 5	15 − 6	15 − 7	15 − 8	15 − 9
16 − 1	16 − 4	16 − 0	16 − 2	16 − 6
16 − 7	16 − 9	16 − 3	16 − 5	16 − 8
16 − 16	15 − 15	16 − 10	16 − 12	15 − 13

21

Secret Code

To find the answer, subtract the numbers, write the difference, and write the letter or punctuation mark above the correct difference below.

What Did The Math Book Say To The Other Math Book?

! 15 – 0 = ___   **,** 16 – 5 = ___   **B** 15 – 7 = ___

E 15 – 15 = ___   **G** 16 – 14 = ___   **R** 15 – 12 = ___

I 15 – 9 = ___   **T** 16 – 12 = ___   **M** 16 – 3 = ___

S 16 – 15 = ___   **V** 15 – 8 = ___   **E** 16 – 6 = ___

L 16 – 7 = ___   **O** 15 – 10 = ___   **P** 16 – 4 = ___

O 16 – 11 = ___

ANSWER

___ ___ ___ ___   ___ ___ ___
6   11   7   0   2   5   4

___ ___ ___ ___ ___ ___ ___ ___ ___
12   3   5   8   9   10   13   1   15

Minuends 15, 16

©2011 Twin Sisters IP, LLC. All Rights Reserved.

Minuend 17

$$\begin{array}{r} 17 \\ -\ 0 \\ \hline \end{array} \qquad \begin{array}{r} 17 \\ -\ 1 \\ \hline \end{array} \qquad \begin{array}{r} 17 \\ -\ 2 \\ \hline \end{array} \qquad \begin{array}{r} 17 \\ -\ 3 \\ \hline \end{array} \qquad \begin{array}{r} 17 \\ -\ 4 \\ \hline \end{array}$$

$$\begin{array}{r} 17 \\ -\ 5 \\ \hline \end{array} \qquad \begin{array}{r} 17 \\ -\ 6 \\ \hline \end{array} \qquad \begin{array}{r} 17 \\ -\ 7 \\ \hline \end{array} \qquad \begin{array}{r} 17 \\ -\ 8 \\ \hline \end{array} \qquad \begin{array}{r} 17 \\ -\ 9 \\ \hline \end{array}$$

$$\begin{array}{r} 17 \\ -\ 1 \\ \hline \end{array} \qquad \begin{array}{r} 17 \\ -\ 4 \\ \hline \end{array} \qquad \begin{array}{r} 17 \\ -\ 0 \\ \hline \end{array} \qquad \begin{array}{r} 17 \\ -\ 2 \\ \hline \end{array} \qquad \begin{array}{r} 17 \\ -\ 6 \\ \hline \end{array}$$

$$\begin{array}{r} 17 \\ -\ 7 \\ \hline \end{array} \qquad \begin{array}{r} 17 \\ -\ 9 \\ \hline \end{array} \qquad \begin{array}{r} 17 \\ -\ 3 \\ \hline \end{array} \qquad \begin{array}{r} 17 \\ -\ 5 \\ \hline \end{array} \qquad \begin{array}{r} 17 \\ -\ 8 \\ \hline \end{array}$$

$$\begin{array}{r} 17 \\ -\ 15 \\ \hline \end{array} \qquad \begin{array}{r} 17 \\ -\ 17 \\ \hline \end{array} \qquad \begin{array}{r} 17 \\ -\ 10 \\ \hline \end{array} \qquad \begin{array}{r} 17 \\ -\ 12 \\ \hline \end{array} \qquad \begin{array}{r} 17 \\ -\ 13 \\ \hline \end{array}$$

Minuend 18

18 − 0	18 − 1	18 − 2	18 − 3	18 − 4
18 − 5	18 − 6	18 − 7	18 − 8	18 − 9
18 − 1	18 − 4	18 − 0	18 − 2	18 − 18
18 − 7	18 − 9	18 − 3	18 − 5	18 − 8
18 − 18	18 − 5	18 − 7	18 − 4	18 − 1

Follow My Lead

Follow my lead. Follow my lead,
as we learn the hard facts of eighteen.
Follow my lead. Follow my lead.
It's time to listen and repeat.

18 - 1 is 17
18 - 2 is 16
18 - 3 is 15

18 - 1 is 17
18 - 2 is 16
18 - 3 is 15

18 - 4 is 14
18 - 5 is 13
18 - 6 is 12

18 - 4 is 14
18 - 5 is 13
18 - 6 is 12

Say them with me. Say them with me,
as we learn the hard facts of eighteen.
Say them with me. Say them with me.
It's time to listen and repeat.

18 - 1 is 17
18 - 4 is 14
18 - 7 is 11

18 - 2 is 16
18 - 5 is 13
18 - 8 is 10

18 - 3 is 15
18 - 6 is 12
18 - 9 is 9

25

18 Sentence Search

Find and circle the subtraction sentences with the minuend 18. Place a − or = sign between the numbers to complete the subtraction sentence. The numbers and differences may be horizontal or vertical.

18	18	18	18	18	18	18	18	18	18
− 0	− 1	− 2	− 3	− 4	− 5	− 6	− 7	− 8	− 9

18	18	18	18	18	18	18	18	18
− 10	− 11	− 12	− 13	− 14	− 15	− 16	− 17	− 18

18 − 9 = 9			18	14	4	17	18	6	12
13	18	12	6	11	12	18	16	2	2
3	18	0	18	5	18	2	18	13	5
18	3	18	10	8	15	16	18	16	2
7	10	18	18	0	7	18	7	6	0
11	12	10	1	9	14	18	3	15	12
3	7	18	17	1	18	5	13	14	10
12	18	11	7	3	7	18	15	3	8
12	18	11	7	3	7	18	15	3	8
18	4	14	1	16	18	8	10	4	0

26

©2011 Twin Sisters IP, LLC. All Rights Reserved.

Target Practice

Complete the targets by subtracting each minuend.

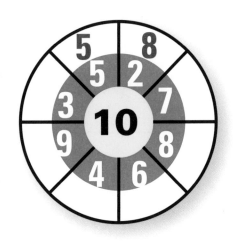 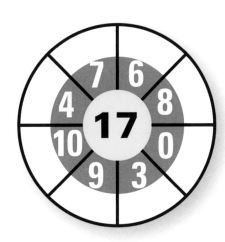 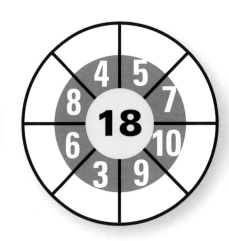

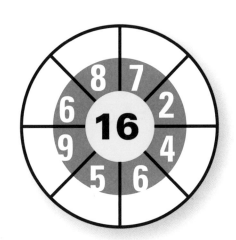 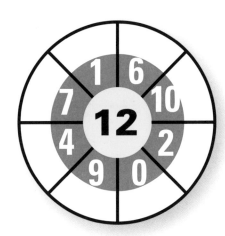 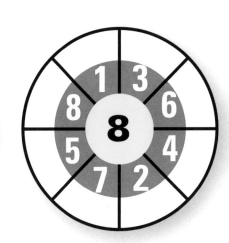

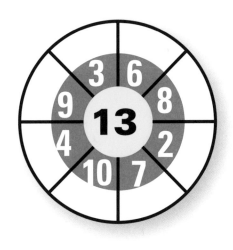 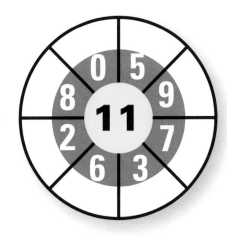 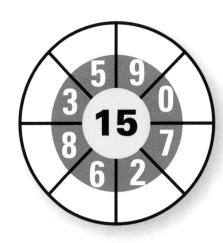

27

Subtraction Review

Solve the problem. Fill in the circle next to the correct answer.

$8 - 6 =$
- ○ 4
- ○ 2
- ○ 1

$5 - 2 =$
- ○ 3
- ○ 4
- ○ 2

$10 - 4 =$
- ○ 4
- ○ 6
- ○ 5

$12 - 5 =$
- ○ 7
- ○ 5
- ○ 6

$9 - 3 =$
- ○ 4
- ○ 5
- ○ 6

$14 - 7 =$
- ○ 7
- ○ 6
- ○ 8

$17 - 8 =$
- ○ 9
- ○ 7
- ○ 8

$13 - 9 =$
- ○ 8
- ○ 4
- ○ 3

$7 - 3 =$
- ○ 10
- ○ 3
- ○ 4

$15 - 5 =$
- ○ 11
- ○ 10
- ○ 9

$6 - 1 =$
- ○ 5
- ○ 2
- ○ 4

$12 - 7 =$
- ○ 6
- ○ 5
- ○ 7

$11 - 4 =$
- ○ 7
- ○ 6
- ○ 8

$16 - 8 =$
- ○ 8
- ○ 9
- ○ 7

$18 - 9 =$
- ○ 7
- ○ 9
- ○ 6

Subtraction Review

Solve the problem. Fill in the circle next to the correct answer.

$9 - 1 =$ ○ 7 ○ 9 ○ 8	$2 - 0 =$ ○ 2 ○ 0 ○ 1	$7 - 7 =$ ○ 6 ○ 7 ○ 0
$14 - 9 =$ ○ 5 ○ 9 ○ 6	$12 - 6 =$ ○ 6 ○ 5 ○ 2	$8 - 4 =$ ○ 4 ○ 5 ○ 2
$3 - 1 =$ ○ 1 ○ 2 ○ 3	$5 - 2 =$ ○ 3 ○ 2 ○ 4	$16 - 9 =$ ○ 8 ○ 9 ○ 7
$13 - 5 =$ ○ 8 ○ 9 ○ 6	$11 - 10 =$ ○ 0 ○ 1 ○ 2	$4 - 1 =$ ○ 3 ○ 2 ○ 0
$6 - 5 =$ ○ 1 ○ 6 ○ 2	$10 - 8 =$ ○ 3 ○ 1 ○ 2	$15 - 3 =$ ○ 11 ○ 12 ○ 10

-1
-2
-3
-4
-5
-6
-7
-8
-9
-10
-11
-12
-13

29

Subtraction Tic Tac Toe

Draw a standard tic tac toe grid. Instead of using **X**s and **O**s, players use the numbers 0 through 9 or 0 through 12. Each number 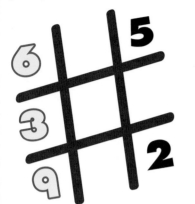 can be used only once during a game. The object of the game is to complete any row, column or diagonal so that the difference of two of the three numbers equals the third number. The first move may **NOT** be in the center; the second and subsequent moves, however, can be anywhere on the board.

Subtraction Tic Tac Toe

31

Match The Problems

Subtract each problem. Then draw a line to match the problem with the same answer.

12 - 6 =

10 - 5 =

14 - 7 =

8 - 4 =

9 - 9 =

17 - 10 =

11 - 8 =

11 - 5 =

5 - 1 =

10 - 7 =

13 - 8 =

18 - 18 =

Greater Than, Less Than or Equal To

Compare and write > (greater than), < (less than),
or = (equal) in the circle.

6 - 3 ◯ 4 - 4   2 - 2 ◯ 1 - 1

10 - 4 ◯ 8 - 7   3 - 2 ◯ 4 - 2

8 - 3 ◯ 5 - 0   8 - 3 ◯ 10 - 4

10 - 3 ◯ 10 - 5   5 - 5 ◯ 6 - 2

4 - 3 ◯ 5 - 2   8 - 4 ◯ 6 - 5

8 - 1 ◯ 10 - 7   10 - 1 ◯ 10 - 2

15 - 6 ◯ 8 - 2   8 - 1 ◯ 5 - 2

33

Greater Than, Less Than or Equal To

Compare and write > (greater than), < (less than),
or = (equal) in the circle.

17 - 10 ◯ 18 -7   15 - 6 ◯ 10 - 1

16 - 15 ◯ 6 - 2   15 - 7 ◯ 16 - 5

15 - 15 ◯ 16 - 6   16 - 7 ◯ 17 - 10

17 - 12 ◯ 18 - 15   17 - 1 ◯ 18 - 0

16 - 6 ◯ 18 - 7   16 - 3 ◯ 15 - 1

16 - 10 ◯ 15 - 6   15 - 6 ◯ 17 - 8

17 - 5 ◯ 15 - 7   17 - 4 ◯ 15 - 1

Subtraction Table Race 1 - 10

Time yourself to see how quickly you can complete the **Subtraction Table**! Before completing the chart, you may want to **photocopy** the page so that you can practice many times! For more fun, play this game with one or more friends. The first player fills in any square on the **Subtraction Table**. The next player fills in another square. It is important to watch carefully what the other players write; if a player makes a mistake, another player may correct it on his or her turn. How quickly can you fill in all the squares?

—	1	2	3	4	5	6	7	8	9	10
1										
2										
3										
4										
5										
6										
7										
8										
9										
10										

35

Subtraction Table Race 10 - 18

Time yourself to see how quickly you can complete the **Subtraction Table**! Before completing the chart, you may want to **photocopy** the page so that you can practice many times! For more fun, play this game with one or more friends. The first player fills in any square on the **Subtraction Table**. The next player fills in another square. It is important to watch carefully what the other players write; if a player makes a mistake, another player may correct it on his or her turn. How quickly can you fill in all the squares?

−	10	11	12	13	14	15	16	17	18
10									
11									
12									
13									
14									
15									
16									
17									
18									

Problem Solving

Read the story problem. Then write the subtraction problem to solve each problem.

1. Katie played 12 volleyball games. Her team won 9 games. How many games did Katie's team lose during the season?   □ − □ = □

2. There were 12 bunnies at the County Fair. Six bunnies were sold. How many bunnies were left?   □ − □ = □

3. Mrs. Smith had 15 balloons. She gave 9 balloons away. How many balloons did Mrs. Smith have left?   □ − □ = □

4. Tom was carrying 10 plates to the table. He dropped all the plates but only 2 broke. How many plates did not break?   □ − □ = □

5. Tyler has 16 video games. He sold eight to a friend. How many video games will Tyler have left?   □ − □ = □

6. The football team played 15 games. They lost 4 games. How many games did the team win?   □ − □ = □

7. Morgan bought 9 pieces of candy. She gave 6 pieces of candy to her friends. How many pieces of candy did Morgan eat?   □ − □ = □

BONUS Problem

Todd ran 5 miles on Monday and Tuesday. He ran 8 miles on Wednesday and Thursday. How many more miles did Todd run on Wednesday and Thursday than he ran on Monday and Tuesday?   □ − □ = □

Real Life Problem Solving

1. Jacob invited 12 friends to his party. Eight friends attended Jacob's party. How many of the friends he invited did not attend Jacob's party?

2. Emily and nine other girls went out to dinner. Six girls ordered pizza. The other girls ordered cheeseburgers. How many ordered cheeseburgers?

3. Twelve skateboarders entered the skateboarding competition. Five skateboarders attend the same school. How many skateboarders attend other schools?

4. Tiffany and her mother bought 8 pairs of jeans at the mall. They returned four pairs of jeans to the mall. How many jeans did Tiffany and her mother keep?

5. The company hired 18 new employees. Nine new employees are women. How many new employees are men?

6. Sam's baseball team won 18 games this season. They lost 7 games. How many more games did Sam's team win than it lost?

7. Scientists predict 17 tropical storms this season. The scientists also predict that 8 of these tropical storms will develop into hurricanes. How many tropical storms are not expected to develop into hurricanes?

8. Eleven boys and 14 girls visited the science museum. How many more girls than boys visited the science museum?

Name: _____ Time [:] Correct [/25]

$$\begin{array}{r}10\\-5\\\hline\end{array}\qquad\begin{array}{r}9\\-6\\\hline\end{array}\qquad\begin{array}{r}2\\-2\\\hline\end{array}\qquad\begin{array}{r}5\\-3\\\hline\end{array}\qquad\begin{array}{r}3\\-1\\\hline\end{array}$$

$$\begin{array}{r}7\\-6\\\hline\end{array}\qquad\begin{array}{r}6\\-4\\\hline\end{array}\qquad\begin{array}{r}4\\-2\\\hline\end{array}\qquad\begin{array}{r}1\\-0\\\hline\end{array}\qquad\begin{array}{r}8\\-7\\\hline\end{array}$$

$$\begin{array}{r}4\\-1\\\hline\end{array}\qquad\begin{array}{r}3\\-3\\\hline\end{array}\qquad\begin{array}{r}5\\-0\\\hline\end{array}\qquad\begin{array}{r}7\\-4\\\hline\end{array}\qquad\begin{array}{r}10\\-8\\\hline\end{array}$$

$$\begin{array}{r}1\\-1\\\hline\end{array}\qquad\begin{array}{r}2\\-0\\\hline\end{array}\qquad\begin{array}{r}6\\-3\\\hline\end{array}\qquad\begin{array}{r}9\\-6\\\hline\end{array}\qquad\begin{array}{r}8\\-4\\\hline\end{array}$$

$$\begin{array}{r}8\\-5\\\hline\end{array}\qquad\begin{array}{r}3\\-2\\\hline\end{array}\qquad\begin{array}{r}2\\-1\\\hline\end{array}\qquad\begin{array}{r}4\\-3\\\hline\end{array}\qquad\begin{array}{r}10\\-10\\\hline\end{array}$$

Name: _____ **Time** [:] **Correct** [/25]

$$\begin{array}{r} 10 \\ -\ 5 \\ \hline \end{array} \qquad \begin{array}{r} 9 \\ -\ 6 \\ \hline \end{array} \qquad \begin{array}{r} 8 \\ -\ 2 \\ \hline \end{array} \qquad \begin{array}{r} 6 \\ -\ 3 \\ \hline \end{array} \qquad \begin{array}{r} 7 \\ -\ 1 \\ \hline \end{array}$$

$$\begin{array}{r} 2 \\ -\ 2 \\ \hline \end{array} \qquad \begin{array}{r} 3 \\ -\ 1 \\ \hline \end{array} \qquad \begin{array}{r} 4 \\ -\ 2 \\ \hline \end{array} \qquad \begin{array}{r} 1 \\ -\ 0 \\ \hline \end{array} \qquad \begin{array}{r} 5 \\ -\ 3 \\ \hline \end{array}$$

$$\begin{array}{r} 8 \\ -\ 1 \\ \hline \end{array} \qquad \begin{array}{r} 7 \\ -\ 4 \\ \hline \end{array} \qquad \begin{array}{r} 5 \\ -\ 0 \\ \hline \end{array} \qquad \begin{array}{r} 10 \\ -\ 8 \\ \hline \end{array} \qquad \begin{array}{r} 9 \\ -\ 7 \\ \hline \end{array}$$

$$\begin{array}{r} 1 \\ -\ 1 \\ \hline \end{array} \qquad \begin{array}{r} 2 \\ -\ 0 \\ \hline \end{array} \qquad \begin{array}{r} 6 \\ -\ 3 \\ \hline \end{array} \qquad \begin{array}{r} 3 \\ -\ 2 \\ \hline \end{array} \qquad \begin{array}{r} 4 \\ -\ 4 \\ \hline \end{array}$$

$$\begin{array}{r} 5 \\ -\ 5 \\ \hline \end{array} \qquad \begin{array}{r} 4 \\ -\ 3 \\ \hline \end{array} \qquad \begin{array}{r} 8 \\ -\ 5 \\ \hline \end{array} \qquad \begin{array}{r} 7 \\ -\ 2 \\ \hline \end{array} \qquad \begin{array}{r} 10 \\ -\ 10 \\ \hline \end{array}$$

40

18 −7	15 −4	16 −9	11 −6	14 −8
12 −6	10 −9	13 −5	17 −3	10 −9
16 −7	14 −8	11 −9	12 −4	10 −8
18 −9	12 −6	10 −7	13 −5	17 −8
11 −5	12 −2	14 −1	16 −9	15 −7

41

$$15 - 9 \qquad 12 - 7 \qquad 18 - 8 \qquad 16 - 5 \qquad 17 - 9$$

$$14 - 6 \qquad 9 - 9 \qquad 10 - 7 \qquad 13 - 9 \qquad 11 - 6$$

$$12 - 6 \qquad 7 - 5 \qquad 11 - 9 \qquad 10 - 4 \qquad 4 - 0$$

$$11 - 3 \qquad 14 - 9 \qquad 9 - 7 \qquad 18 - 9 \qquad 3 - 2$$

$$10 - 5 \qquad 5 - 2 \qquad 16 - 1 \qquad 13 - 3 \qquad 3 - 1$$

Name: _____ **Time** [:] **Correct** [/50]

1 −1	2 −1	5 −2	3 −1	3 −2
3 −3	4 −1	4 −3	1 −1	3 −1
3 −2	5 −4	2 −2	4 −3	5 −0
2 −1	4 −2	5 −5	2 −2	1 −1
4 −3	3 −3	4 −1	3 −2	5 −1
5 −0	5 −4	3 −1	2 −1	1 −0
3 −0	2 −2	4 −3	5 −2	5 −3
2 −1	3 −3	5 −1	5 −4	1 −1
4 −4	2 −0	3 −1	5 −0	1 −0
2 −2	3 −1	4 −2	5 −3	4 −2

43

Name: _____ **Time** | : | **Correct** | /50

4 −1	3 −1	2 −2	5 −1	1 −1
2 −0	1 −1	3 −3	5 −1	4 −1
5 −2	2 −1	3 −2	4 −3	1 −0
1 −0	4 −2	5 −5	3 −2	2 −1
4 −3	3 −3	4 −1	3 −2	5 −1
2 −0	1 −1	5 −5	4 −3	4 −4
3 −0	2 −2	4 −3	5 −2	2 −0
2 −1	5 −3	4 −1	2 −2	3 −1
4 −4	3 −0	1 −0	5 −5	4 −3
4 −2	5 −1	3 −2	3 −3	2 −2

Name: _____ **Time** ☐ **:** ☐ **Correct** ☐ **/50**

9 −1	6 −3	8 −2	10 −4	7 −6
6 −3	7 −1	9 −3	8 −1	10 −1
10 −2	8 −4	6 −2	7 −3	9 −0
7 −1	6 −2	10 −5	9 −4	8 −5
6 −3	10 −3	7 −5	6 −2	10 −1
10 −0	7 −4	9 −1	8 −7	8 −0
9 −6	10 −2	6 −3	7 −2	8 −3
6 −1	8 −3	7 −1	10 −4	9 −1
7 −4	9 −0	10 −1	8 −0	7 −0
10 −2	7 −1	9 −2	8 −3	6 −2

45

Name: _____ **Time** | : | **Correct** | /50

6 −1	7 −3	8 −2	10 −4	9 −6
10 −3	9 −1	7 −3	6 −1	8 −1
8 −2	10 −4	9 −2	8 −3	7 −0
7 −1	8 −2	10 −5	7 −4	6 −5
9 −3	6 −3	6 −5	9 −2	10 −1
10 −8	7 −5	9 −5	8 −4	8 −2
9 −6	10 −7	6 −6	7 −6	8 −6
6 −6	8 −8	7 −3	10 −1	9 −0
7 −2	9 −3	10 −4	8 −7	7 −6
10 −5	7 −2	9 −6	8 −2	6 −1

Name: _____ **Time** [:] **Correct** [/50]

18 −1	17 −3	16 −2	15 −5	14 −7
9 −4	10 −6	11 −8	12 −9	13 −5
8 −1	7 −3	6 −1	5 −4	4 −2
16 −9	18 −9	1 −0	2 −1	3 −3
17 −8	15 −6	13 −9	14 −9	12 −6
7 −5	9 −5	8 −3	10 −2	11 −7
6 −6	4 −3	5 −4	3 −2	5 −4
18 −3	16 −4	12 −5	15 −4	17 −7
13 −7	14 −6	10 −5	8 −5	11 −9
7 −2	6 −3	4 −2	5 −4	3 −2

Name: _____ **Time** [:]   **Correct** [/50]

11 −1	5 −3	13 −2	13 −5	14 −7
8 −4	16 −6	17 −8	18 −9	15 −9
1 −1	10 −3	9 −1	8 −4	7 −2
15 −6	17 −9	15 −0	3 −1	5 −3
16 −9	14 −7	12 −5	13 −9	11 −5
6 −5	8 −5	7 −3	9 −2	14 −5
5 −3	3 −1	4 −4	2 −1	4 −3
17 −3	15 −2	11 −2	14 −3	16 −4
12 −6	13 −5	9 −4	7 −5	10 −9
6 −2	5 −1	3 −2	4 −1	2 −2

48